Gnomes Games

Based on the book GNOMES, published by Harry N. Abrams, Inc.
© 1976 UNIEBOEK B.V. Text by Wil Huygen, Illustrated by Rien Poortvliet

Games Designed by
LARRY EVANS

TROUBADOR PRESS SAN FRANCISCO

LITTLE GNOME FACTS

Gnomes are little people who live, for the most part, in houses built under trees in the forest. They are about 15cm. tall (including their caps), and live to a ripe old age of 400 years. Their associations with the animals of the forest are close. However, they have a hard time accepting polecats because the cats paralyze frogs and save them for later eating.

Gnomes are night creatures and rise for breakfast in the early evening. Some of the other night creatures that share the forest with the gnomes are elves, goblins, trolls, dwarfs, river spirits and uldras. Gnomes don't have much to do with these creatures except for the trolls. Trolls are stupid, primitive, distrustful and ugly (they smell bad too). They have certain magic power over gnomes, but only in their caves.

Gnomes live with their parents until they are 100 years old. About that time, the male begins to think of marriage. On the gnomes' honeymoon, the couple visits the gnome king and queen. Usually 12 months later a pair of twins is born to the gnome couple. The twins may be two boys, two girls or a boy and a girl. Gnomes *love* to play games and work puzzles. Contained within this volume is a variety of the games most often played by the gnomes. This selection of puzzles was made with the expert help of Tomte Haroldson, a 379-year-old gnome from Holland, who strongly felt that something good might come from this effort.

Library of Congress Cataloging in Publication Data
Evans, Larry, 1939-
   Gnomes games.

   SUMMARY: Includes hidden picture puzzles, mazes, cryptic codes, and many other games featuring the characters from the book *Gnomes*.
   1. Games. 2. Puzzles. 3. Huygen, Wil.
Leven en werken van de kabouter. [1. Games.
2. Puzzles] I. Huygen, Wil. Leven en werken van de kabouter. II. Poortvliet, Rien. III. Title.
GV1201.E85   793.73   80-24935
ISBN 0-89844-020-3

GNOME BALANCING ACT

A dwarf balances with a gnome and a goblin. A gnome balances with a goblin and a troll. Two dwarfs balance with three trolls.

QUESTION

How many goblins would balance with a gnome?

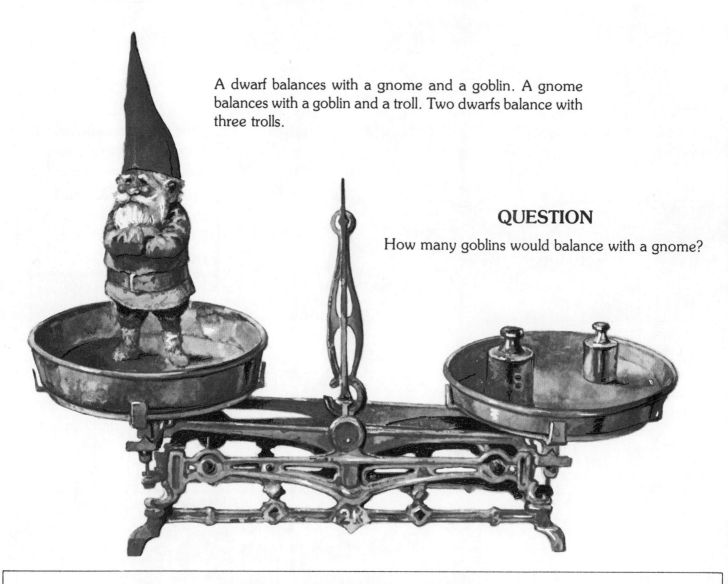

THE GNOMES' TUNNEL

Two gnomes had spent the night digging a tunnel. At daybreak they both climbed out to go home. One had a dirty face and the other a clean face. The gnome with the dirty face went right home while the gnome with the clean face stopped to wash before going home. **Why?**

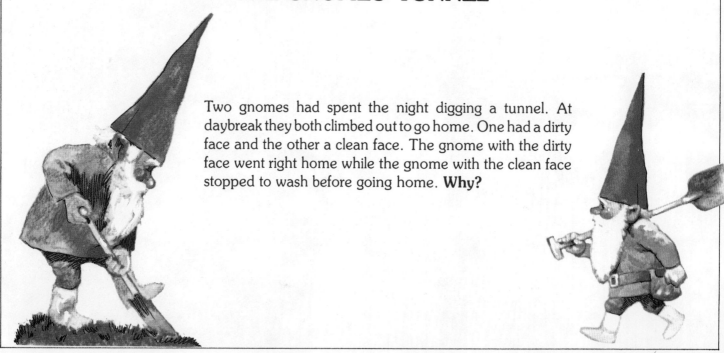

Find seven differences between the top and the bottom picture.

THE TOOL BOX

Can you tell without measuring, just how many tools will fit in the gnome's tool box and how many won't?

GNOME GNONSENSE

- What is the difference between a seamstress and a groom?

- What is always behind time?

- What is the largest room in the world?

- How do bees get rid of their honey?

Which silhouette most closely matches the dwarf at the top of the page?

THE OLDEST GNOME

The oldest gnome in the forest is 480 years old. He is now twice as old as his nephew was when the old gnome was in his prime. How old is the nephew?

THE CELEBRATION

Every once in a while, three gnomes, Thym, Imp and Tomte, celebrate a good day in the woods by having dinner at Imp's house. After dinner one morning, they asked Imp's wife, Lisa, to bring them a dessert bowl of hazelnuts. While waiting for the hazelnuts to be served, all three gnomes had a generous amount of spiced gin and promptly fell asleep. After a while, Thym awoke, saw the bowl of nuts, ate his equal share and went back to sleep. Tomte then awakened and ate what he *thought* was his equal share and fell asleep again. Finally, Imp woke up, ate what he considered *his* equal share of the remainder, then he too went back to sleep. When the gnomes all awakened later they discovered that eight hazelnuts were left. How many hazelnuts were in the bowl originally?

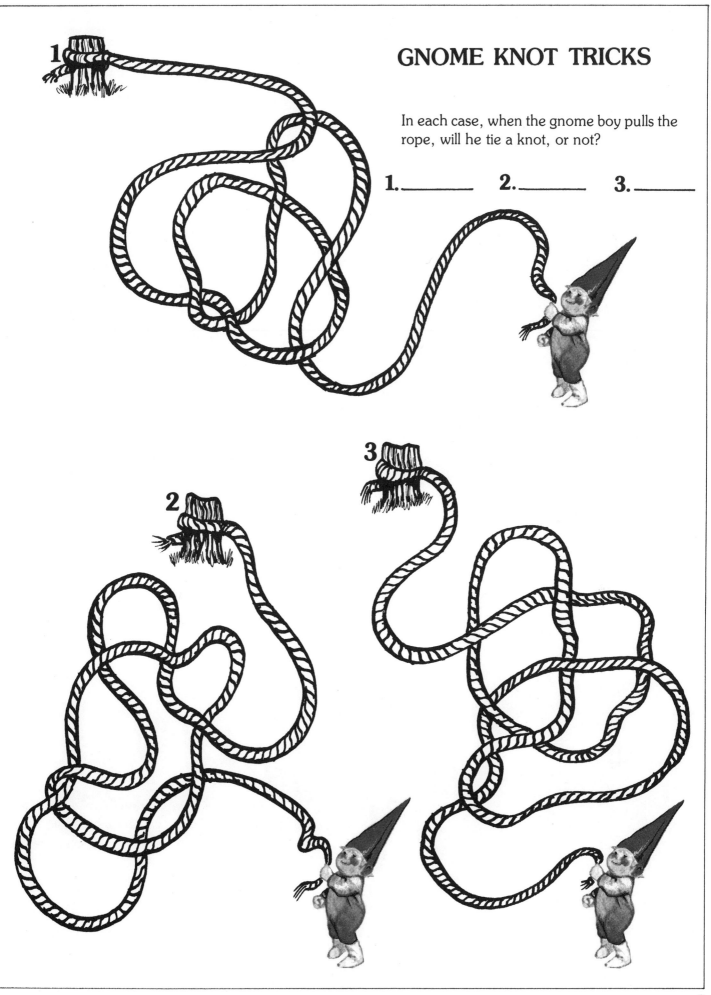

GNOME KNOT TRICKS

In each case, when the gnome boy pulls the rope, will he tie a knot, or not?

1._____ 2._____ 3._____

THE TROLL'S TRICK QUESTIONS

Is there a law against a gnome marrying his widow's sister?

Gnome Tomte leaves his home traveling one kilometer per hour. Troll Pimple leaves his cave traveling 1.5 kph. When they meet, which will be the closest to the cave, Tomte or Pimple?

If a gnome is on top of a mountain with a live goose, what would be the quickest way for him to get down?

A gnome has a rope that is two meters long tied to his ankle. How can he reach a basket of berries six meters away?

If it takes four minutes for a gnome to fry an egg, how many minutes does it take him to fry two eggs?

HIDDEN GNOMES

Six little gnome boys have hidden themselves in the picture on the opposite page. There are two older gnomes there too. I can see one, can you see the other?

THE THREE BASKETS

There are three baskets of fruit and nuts on this page. One is labeled **HAZELNUTS,** one is labeled **BLACKBERRIES,** and one is labeled **HAZELNUTS & BLACKBERRIES**. Each one is incorrect. The gnome may take one item from each basket (no peeking). How can the gnome label the baskets correctly?

THE BIRTHDAY CODE

High upon a birthday tree is carved a cryptic code...or is it? Can you figure out what the next two letters should be? Imp has been up the tree at least ten times and he still can't figure it out.

H	n	v	U	L	O	w	j	b	i
Q	I	o	w	H	J	v	d	I	U
L	v	w	y	H	Q	c	V	L	a
H	N	h	L	i	W	j	k	H	I
V	q	u	W	E	L	u	h	e	J
P	V	j	a	H	S	Q	e	q	i
U	v	C	i	l	W	r	j	u	e
T	Q	L	j	F	i	q	r	w	O
w	m	L	a	J	g	H	N		
V	O	u	m	E					

Black out every letter that shows up more than **six** times.
Then see if you can read the important gnome message.

Assume that the following statements are true:

1. All gnomes smile.
2. Some gnomes are house gnomes.
3. All farm gnomes are conservative.
4. Some house gnomes are conservative.
5. All house gnomes are in fact gnomes.

From the list above, which of the following statements are true and which are false?

1. All house gnomes smile.
2. Some house gnomes are not conservative.

3. Some gnomes are not house gnomes.
4. All smiling gnomes are farm gnomes.
5. All farm gnomes that are conservative, smile.
6. All smiling house gnomes are conservative.
7. Gnomes that are not conservative are not farm gnomes.
8. All smiling farm gnomes are conservative.

Which is the least like the others?
BARLEY   WHEAT   HAY   OATS   RICE

GNOME REBUS

Discover an amazing fact about gnomes by solving this rebus.

		G		
		N		
G	N	O	M	E
		M		
		E		

GNOME WORD SQUARE

The words in this square read the same horizontally and vertically. Here are some clues to get you started.
1. Can't see without it.
2. Near the center.
3. **GNOME**
4. Rope fibers (plural)
5. Length of hair.
Don't mind the gnome, he's not laughing at *you*.

THE GOBLIN'S MAZE

The bunny has found a way to run through the maze without meeting the horrid goblin. Help the gnome trace the bunny's path. If you chance to meet the goblin, start all over again.

WHAT A GNOME KNOWS

ꝿꞟꞟꝼꝹꞟꞟꞟꞟꝼꞟꞟ

This ancient rune spells a secret treatment the gnomes use to cure animals of their aches and pains. Can you decipher it?

HIDDEN FOREST CREATURES

Hidden within each sentence below is the name of a creature of the forest. How many can you find (the first one has been solved)?

Gnome wives make great rolls.

Gnomes would end war forever.

There you go, blinking again.

Keep the hazelnuts off the shelf.

Lisa made ermine slippers.

You can take it from me, Olie is over 300 years old.

You can angle for fish or net them

It is not Terry's fault that the tea cup broke.

THE DOWRY CHEST

Gnome Olie wanted to store his hazelnuts in his bride's dowry chest. He had eleven nuts but only ten compartments. His unique solution was to put two hazelnuts in the first compartment. He then put the rest of the nuts away as follows:

Nut three in compartment two
Nut four in compartment three
Nut five in compartment four
Nut six in compartment five
Nut seven in compartment six
Nut eight in compartment seven
Nut nine in compartment eight
Nut ten in compartment nine.

He then opened up the first compartment and took out one of the two hazelnuts he has placed there. He put that nut in compartment ten. He had then stored all of his hazelnuts in their own compartments.
Can you find anything wrong with Olie's plan?

TROLLS

What is the difference between a hungry troll and a gluttonous troll?

THE WEARY TRAVELER

Everyone knows that trolls are malicious and meddlesome, but few people know that if they would chance to meet troll twins, the odds are that one would be a liar and one would tell the truth. This very meeting took place when a cold and lost forest traveler came upon troll twins standing at a fork in the trail. Knowing full well that he could ask only *one* question, what could the traveler ask to guarantee the correct directions?

MISSING TROLL PIECES

In the illustration above, three pieces are missing. Select the correct squares below that complete the picture, then enter the numbers on the lines below.

A _____   B _____   C _____

1   2   3   4   5   6

7   8   9   10   11   12

THE CUCKOO CLOCK

The traditional gnome wedding present given to the groom on his wedding day is the cuckoo clock. This clock however, has the face reversed. Can you tell what time it is?

Which of the following is least like the other four?

COPPER   **BRASS**   **LEAD**   **TIN**   **IRON**

GNOME WORD SEARCH

```
S L L O R T H L M S A B B O W S O V M P F
N B E I O S E V L E N G L K S N R O C A A
O A D F N A U W L F G H O W A T H U I R Z
W O C E M O N G C I S P W T T E N R O H D
B D C O Z H R O Q U E R P E U H I T O B E
A A L M J U T B U M K Y I I A E R S L S E
L E U E G M S L H O A O P L S P I R I T S
L Q F T L E U I F O N F E V Q U A M T A C
H G O B E W O N U R S R S T U S E O W P L
O N B S T V A P T H B A P R I B L M L I O
S H Y A M C O A W S X W L V R T I S M N K
R N H M O E Y C A U S D A O R V M P L E A
E O E T P Y L H L M R Z B P E H O B K C T
R I T G A H L L B A V A G O L T M S T O G
E A W T Y R Z C E O R E L O B I A A S N S
C S I Y E U E B S T H Y M A H O C U R E E
R U N I C R H T R Q M F A M B E Q U E L H
O W S Z M E S B T U R O F I L T G S W A C
S M O U F L O N E O E X T O S U J D K E T
P Q U R T F C G G S Z L P M N I S S E R I
U L L I M W A S A C U P U N C T U R E H W
```

The words below are hidden within the letters above. They may be found horizontally, vertically, diagonally, backward and forward. One example is given.

ELVES	OTTER	SMELL	ALCOVE
RUNIC	ACUPUNCTURE	SNAKES	COW
BLOWPIPES	ACORN	OWL	SNOTGURGLE
HEDGEHOG	GNOME	SNOWBALL	SORCERERS
SEED	HORNET	BEARD	WITCHES
POLECAT	MUSHROOM	TOMTE	~~FAIRIES~~
FROG	SAWMILL	TROLLS	DWARF
MOUFLON	MOLE	THYM	NYMPH
SQUIRREL	TWINS	FOX	GOBLIN
PINECONE	BOLERO	CAMOMILE	SPIRITS
NISSE	HUYGEN	IMP	CAP

THE ART LESSON

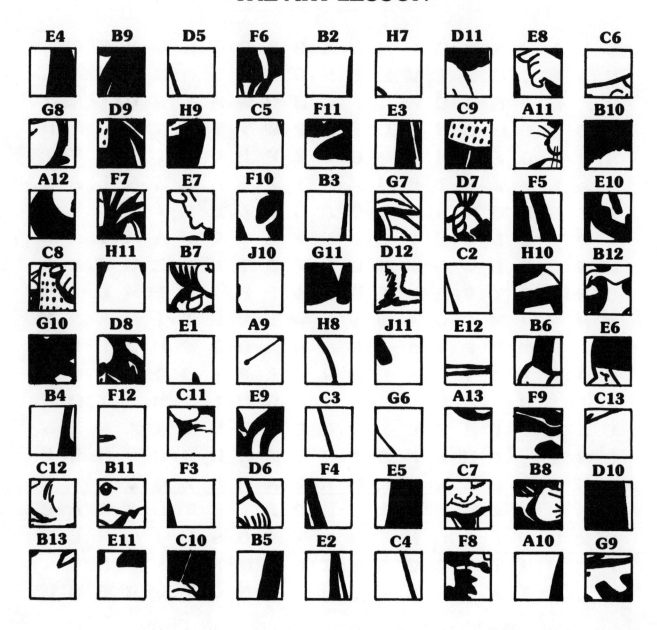

Hidden within the jumbled squares above is a secret gnome drawing. Transfer the shapes in the squares above to their counterparts on the next page. When you have finished, you will have discovered the secret gnome drawing. Then it won't be a secret anymore. Everyone knows that you can't keep a secret from a gnome.

	A	B	C	D	E	F	G	H	J
1									
2									
3									
4									
5									
6									
7									
8									
9									
10									
11									
12									
13									

GNOME GEOMETRY

| | | | |

The gnome has made four marks in his book...
Put **five** more marks to make **ten.**

Is it correct to say, "seven and five **is** thirteen"—or, "seven and five **are** thirteen?"

An incorrect answer sends you down through the trap door into the next question.

A gnome came upon a bridge posted with a sign saying: **WEIGHT LIMIT 310 GRAMS**. The gnome weighs 300 grams and he carries three berries that weigh five grams apiece. He can't throw them across the stream and he can only make one trip across as he is in a hurry.

How will the gnome get himself *and* his berries across the stream?

Which gnome carrying the pheasant chick is the direct opposite of the negative above?

THE MEAD DEW PUZZLES

Gnome Wartje one day decided to ask 100 of his fellow gnomes whether they drank mead dew (fermented honey) or fermented raspberries during supper.
78 said they drank mead dew.
71 said they drank fermented raspberries.
48 said they drank both.
0 said they drank neither.
Gnome Kostja said there was an obvious mistake. Can you find it?

THE SPICED GIN CAPER

One evening Olie Hammerslag was sitting at his dinner table. Before him was a ¾-full cup of spiced gin and a cup ¾ full of mead dew. Absentmindedly, Olie put a spoonful of spiced gin into the cup of mead dew. He then put a spoonful of mead dew (with the spoonful of spiced gin in it) into the spiced gin.
Did Olie have more mead dew in the spiced gin than vice versa, or less?

```
            Q P O N M N O J U T S R Q P Q R S P Q R S T
            R S P M L Q P I V B A Z O I J U T O R W V U
            U T Q N K R G H W X Y N G H K L M N S X Y Z
            V W R O J S F I J K L M F N M L K U T G H I
            Y X S P I T E D C B C D E O H I V J I L F J
            Z A T Q H U V B A A S R Q P G J W X H M K E
            B W U V G K W B Z B T D E F V U E Y G N C D
            Y A W F J X C Y C U C G H W D T F Z O B A
        ←Z Y X E I Y D X W V B J I C X S R Q P E Z
            O P Q D H Z E Y Z A Y Z A B Y Z A B C D Y
            M N R S C G F X B A X K J I H G F H G F E X
  M L K J I J K L M B T U V W C W Q Y L B C D E I T U V W
  N Z F G H N O P A N B L M R S V P M Z A B C D J S R Q P
  O E Y J I M X Y Z A O K Q F T U O N A Z Y X E K L M R O
  D C X W K L W O N M L P J G E J D C B A I W F G N Q S N
  C B A V U T V U T S K J I H D K I E C B H V U T O P T M
  V W B Z O P S W X R Q P O N M L C H D C G F E S Y X U L
  U X C N Y P Q R Y Z V W X Y Z A B G E D I H D R Z W V K
  Y T D M X W V U T S U M L K J I H I F E F J C Q A H I J
  Z E S X L K J I H R T N Q P O I G Q P O N K P B F G R S
  U V W R Y A B I G Q P O R S N F H R C M L O L M E Q L T
  T E F G Q Z C F H G I J K L M E S G D B N B C D P K M U
  S D C B A P E D E F G H Z Y C D T F E M A Z Y E J O N V
  R Q P U O D C B W X Y Z A B X H U K L I H G X I D E F G
  N O V N T R Q A V B C D E F G W V J K J I F W H C B A H
  M W M D E S P Z U A B C D E F G H I B C D E V G D A Z I
  X L C B M N O T Y Z C O N M L K J I A H S T U F E B Y X
  K Y Z A L R S W X Y D X Y Z A W X Y Z G R M N O P Q R W
  J C B K B Q P V A Z W S T U V B C D E F Q L K J        S V
  I D J D C Z O U W V S R L K J I H G F P O N H I        T U
  H E I E H Y N T U U T Q M O P Q R F G K L M G
  G H F G X I M S R Q P O N I H G F E I J D E F
  B F E W J K L O N M L K J I H G E D H C C
  A C D V U T S R Q O N K L J H G F G C B B
  Z Y X W V U T S R P M L K K L F E D C B A←
```

IMP'S GIANT A-B-C MAZE

Race with Imp through the alphabet, starting at **A**. When you reach **Z** start all over with
another **A** until you reach the end. You may go horizontally, vertically and diagonally.

PIMPLE'S ALIBI

In the home of Tomte Haroldson, someone has broken in and smashed his wedding clock. Pimple, the troll, says he can prove he was in his cave between 7 P.M. and 9 P.M., so he couldn't have done it. Can you put the pieces of the clock back together to find out just what time the clock was broken? They fit just like a jigsaw puzzle. Don't cut them out; just put the proper numbers where they belong.

GNOME CYPHER

Each letter in this cypher stands for another. The substitution is consistent throughout.

JLDFFDGC DJ QHH IDJEM BHJ CGHFKJ.

A truth known to all gnomes and night people.

THE MYSTERIOUS BROTHER

A gnome's brother passed away the other day. Strange thing though, the gnome who died had *no* brother.
How was this possible?

Gnome Kostja decided to board up part of his window because it let in too much light. His window was 15cm wide by 15cm tall. After he had boarded up half the window, he was amazed to discover that the remaining half was still square in shape and still measured 15cm high by 15cm wide.
How did gnome Kostja board up the window?

ANOTHER GNOME CYPHER

This cypher is all about wood and just what happens in a fierce storm.

EKU GZEHDY AS KLEBYSY, YEQ'J GJKQY HQYSF K MBDDEM, JZS VBQS BG BQ YKQCSF, AHJ ASSXZ IKP AS GKTSDP GEHCZJ.

Help Imp rearrange the pieces of this funny horse to make the best looking horse he can.

GNOME CRISS-CROSS

All the words below fit into the criss-cross puzzle either horizontally or vertically. They have been arranged in groups to aid your hunt.

3 LETTERS	**4 LETTERS**		**5 LETTERS**	**6 LETTERS**	**8 LETTERS**
JAM	MICE	MOSS	ELVES	SKIING	PORRIDGE
TEA	HOME	HARE	GNOME	ULDRAS	MUSHROOM
HOP	MOLE	AXES	DOWRY	HORNET	PINECONE
POX	TUFT	RODE	TROLL	SHOVEL	**9 LETTERS**
CAT	WELL	MINT	MOREL	PIMPLE	DANDELION
ALE	FELT	ROAD	NYMPH	POTTER	**11 LETTERS**
PEA	PEAT	DIET	MUSIC	**7 LETTERS**	RIVERSPIRIT
OAK	IRIS	BITE	SPICE	GOBLINS	
	NOUN	NEAR	SKATE	HAMSTER	

THE SECRET FOOTPRINT

Discover, if you can, the footprint that best matches the design on the bottom of the boot at the beginning of the puzzle.

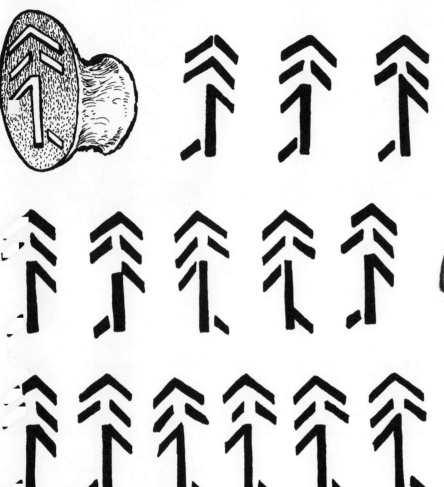

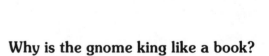

Why is the gnome king like a book?

Which gnome family best matches the silhouette?

GNOME BERRIES

Tomte, Imp and Olie met under Imp's birthday tree and decided to swap some of the contents of their baskets. Tomte first said to Olie, "I'll give you six blackberries for a huckleberry, then you'll have twice as many berries as I have." Imp then said to Tomte, "I will give you 14 blueberries for a huckleberry, then you will have three times as many berries as I have." Olie finally said to Imp, "I'll give you four strawberries for a huckleberry, then you will have six times as many berries as I have."

Can you tell how many berries each gnome had before any exchange was made?

Carved high up in Imp's birthday tree is this strange incomplete word square. Can you add the proper letters so that the square will read the same top to bottom and left to right?

MOTHER GNOME'S MIXED BAG

There are at least 30 words hidden within the rectangular spiral. Starting with the first letter (P) and reading clockwise around the spiral, how many words can you discover?

P	O	L	E	C	A	T	E
O	L	L	A	M	A	G	L
R	N	O	M	E	N	I	F
T	G	E	V	I	D	C	I
S	N	O	L	W	O	R	N
E	R	O	F	R	A	W	D

$$1 \qquad 2 \qquad 3 \qquad 4 \qquad 5$$

GNOME IDENTITY CRISIS

A woodland gnome, a dune gnome, a garden gnome, a farm gnome and a house gnome are having their portrait painted. From the following facts, can you identify each gnome?

1. The house gnome is at one end of the portrait.
2. The dune gnome is not Thym.
3. Olie is in the center (between the woodland gnome and the farm gnome).
4. Tomte is the woodland gnome's cousin.
5. There is nobody at Wartje's right.
6. Thym, who is nearest the flower, lost to the house gnome at bowling yesterday.
7. Tomte stands at Wartje's left.
8. Imp's wife just had twins.

Can you name each gnome and what kind he is?

If Tomte's father is Imp's son, what relation is Tomte to Imp?

Starting anywhere, find the shortest route that the gnome has to take to dig all 17 tunnels that connect the trees. You (and the gnome) may touch each tree as often as you like.

THE TROLL'S SQUARE

This magic square contains five words that read the same horizontally and vertically. Can you guess the proper words from the following clues?

1. Opening on a ship.
2. Halos
3. **Troll**
4. A bovine birthing.
5. Troy's lady.

GNOME'S BOWLING

The ten stacks of letters (bowling pins) each contain the letters of ten six-letter words. The first letter of each word has been circled. After you have unscrambled the spellings, stack the words in the proper sequence, one on top of the other. The final letters of each word will spell out the name of the character pictured on top of this page.

RLS   BOG   REO   BIR   LAC
TO   IN   LO   TR   RD
L (T)___   L (G)___   B (B)___   A (R)___   E (C)___

WGN   GIN   AEU   REL   NNL
SI   DA   UB   OF   EE
A (S)___   I (G)___   R (B)___   W (F)___   F (F)___

<u>S</u> ___ ___ ___ ___ ___ ___ ___ ___ ___

THE TROLL'S LADDER

What are the fewest number of steps the troll has to take to climb this ladder in order to be on the top rung twice and on the ground twice? Every rung is the same height and all must be used the same number of times.

Do you know the difference between a troll's ladder and a regular ladder?

TROLL PIMPLE'S CYPHER

In this cypher, each letter has been substituted for another. The letter coding is consistent even though Pimple fought against it.

TSB CPACSM PD J QMJYDTAM ZYTSS.

Would you say that the caps contain more grey or black felt?

MISSING GNOME PIECES

Three pieces are missing from the drawing of the gnome. Choose which pieces fit the lettered openings and write the letters on the blank lines below.

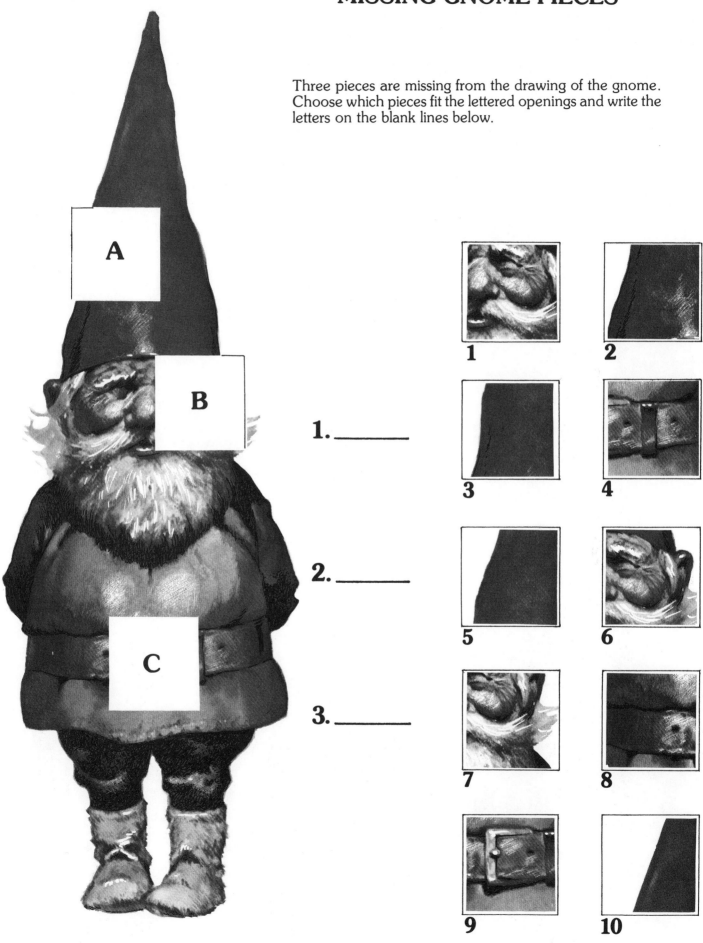

1. _____

2. _____

3. _____

Gnome is to troll as **65943** is to:

A. 87320   B. 95681
C. 40569   D. 82128
     E. 87922

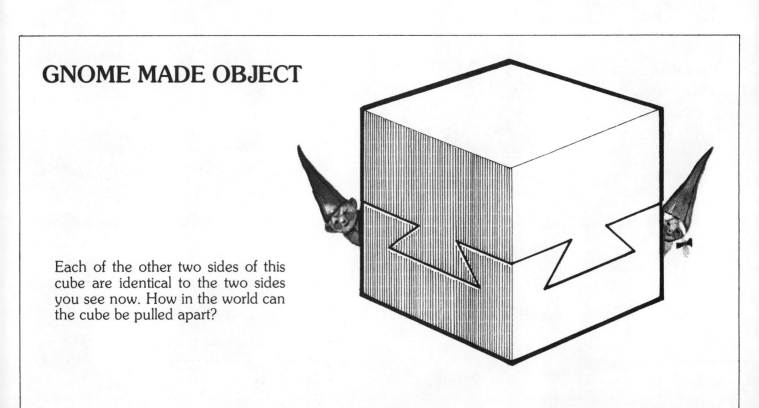

GNOME MADE OBJECT

Each of the other two sides of this cube are identical to the two sides you see now. How in the world can the cube be pulled apart?

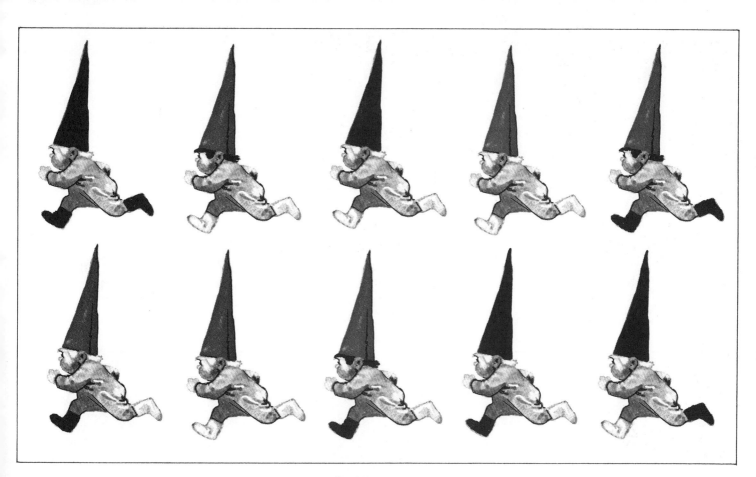

GNOME TWINS

Find the two runners that match; then find the twin gnome boys below.

45

GNOME MONOGRAMS

Each monogram below is a combination of letters that spells the name of an animal that shares the forest with the gnomes.

1

2

3

4

5

6

7

8

9

THE SAWING PIT

The gnomes at the sawing pit have four pieces of wood. Each one is either black or white on one side and each has either a triangle or an oval on the other side. Which ones must you turn over to gain enough information to answer the following question?
Does every black board have an oval on the other side?

THE GNOME MISSING LINK

Only the letters that spell **GNOME** are placed in the puzzle. You must find the proper spots to place the words below.

2 LETTERS	**4 LETTERS**	**5 LETTERS**	**6 LETTERS**	
OH	SHOT	TOOLS	FOREST	
TO	LAST	GLOSS	ULDRAS	
US	BAND	BREAD	LICHEN	
3 LETTERS	GOAT	TROLL	OTTERS	
FIG	ANTS	ROOTS	SECRET	
TUB	NUTS	SWING	**7 LETTERS**	**8 LETTERS**
FUR	TERN	ELVES	CANDLES	SOAPWART
ALE	SONG	REBUS	WILLOWS	PORRIDGE
DOE	TREE	DWARF	TWISTED	PHEASANT
ASH	SOAR	OFTEN	HAMSTER	**9 LETTERS**
HAT	ANTE		RODENTS	RAINWATER
	FAST		HOPPING	SQUIRRELS
			SIBERIA	

A GNOME'S DILEMMA

A gnome is on a square island covered with dry grass and trees. A fire is raging across one end of the island. The wind is blowing toward him at a rapid rate so the fire will overtake the gnome shortly and engulf the entire island. High cliffs block his escape and there appears to be no way for the gnome to save himself. Can you discover how the gnome finally saves himself?

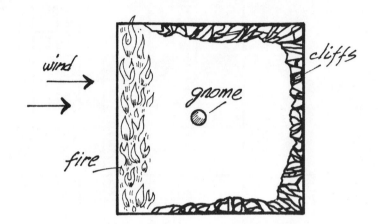

THE CROSS COUNTRY RACE

Gnomes are fast runners and often have running contests. In one cross-country race half of the gnomes who entered dropped out in the first hour. One third of the rest quit in the next 30 minutes. After two hours another quarter of the remaining gnomes dropped out leaving only nine to complete the race.
How many gnomes began the race?

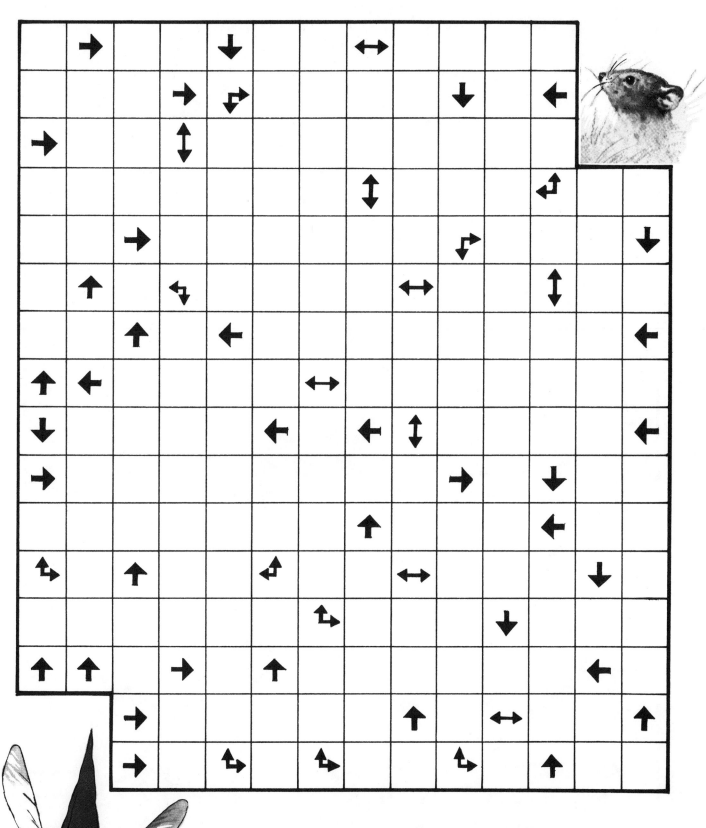

THE ARROW MAZE

The gnome boy must enter the arrow maze at one of the four *in* arrows at the lower left of the puzzle. He must then follow the direction of the arrow until he reaches the next arrow (traveling horizontally or vertically). He then follows *that* arrow's direction to the next, changing direction accordingly, and so on. See how fast you can help the gnome boy flutter his way through the maze to the mouse.

LISA'S QUILT

Gnome Lisa is standing in front of a quilt of her own design. Can you color it with *four* colors so that no colored area touches another of the same color? Use the symbols B, Y, G and R if you don't wish to use color.

GNOME SQUARES

The gnome girl wishes to cut the square in her towel into **six** square pieces. Show her how to do it.

Can you show the gnome how to build a square table out of this piece of wood? Try it with only *two* cuts.

Divide this page with *three* straight lines so that each wooden bunny and each gnome twin occupies his own space. No line may enter this paragraph.

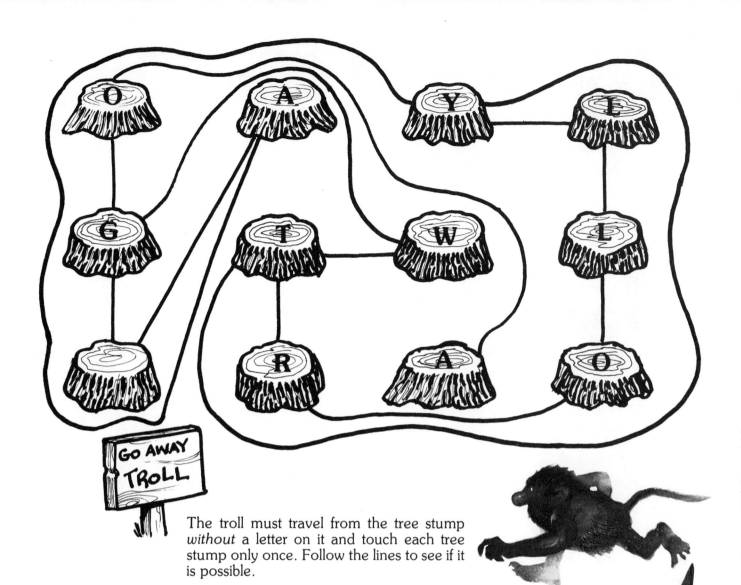

The troll must travel from the tree stump *without* a letter on it and touch each tree stump only once. Follow the lines to see if it is possible.

THE LIFE OF A GNOME

The average life of a gnome is 300 years or more. The list below describes several historical events. If a gnome just turned 300 in 1980, how many of these events would have occurred during his lifetime?

1. The rule of James V of Scotland
2. The reign in Russia of Peter the Great
3. The destruction of the Spanish Armada by England
4. The great fire of London
5. The reign of Louis XIV of France
6. The printing of the first bible by Johann Gutenberg
7. The reign, in Austria, of Maria Theresa
8. The founding of Boston
9. Pennsylvania charted by William Penn
10. Champlain sails up the St. Lawrence river and takes possession for France.
11. Execution of Charles I in London
12. The signing of the Magna Carta by King John at Runnymede

A GNOME'S AGE

Tomte's son is five times as old as his daughter and his wife is five times as old as his son and he is twice as old as his wife. His mother is as old as all of them put together and is celebrating her 81st birthday. How old is Tomte's son?

A gnome keeps busy while using the bathroom. Many artistic objects are created during this time. While the gnome is busy can you find *seven* differences between the pictures?

```
G N O M E G G N O M E G G G G
G N O M E O N G O E G N O N N
G N O M E G O N M E O O O O
N N E M O N G O N M G E N M E
O G O E E O N M E N N M G M I
M G N M G M O E O N M O O O E
E N G N E E M G N O G N N N I
G O O G G N E M O N G G O G O
N M G N N G G N O M E M E N I
E E O N E O N M E G E M O N G
N M E N O M E O N G N O M E I
E M O                 N E N O N G O
N N                   E N E O M G I
G O                   G N O M M N E
```

How many ways—forward, backward, vertically, horizontally and diagonally—can you find the word: **GNOME**

55

GNOME RELATIONS

I am Lisa.
Tomte and Imp
are my nephews.

I am Wartje.
Tomte and Imp
are my cousins.

I am Elsa.
Imp and Wartje are
my nephews.

I am Tomte.
Imp is my son.

I am Alice.
Wartje is my
nephew.

I am Imp.

How are the three gnome
women related to each
other?

What is the best way to make a coat last?

THE ULDRA'S PUZZLES

The uldras are creatures found only in Lapland. They resemble gnomes but are somewhat larger and colorless.

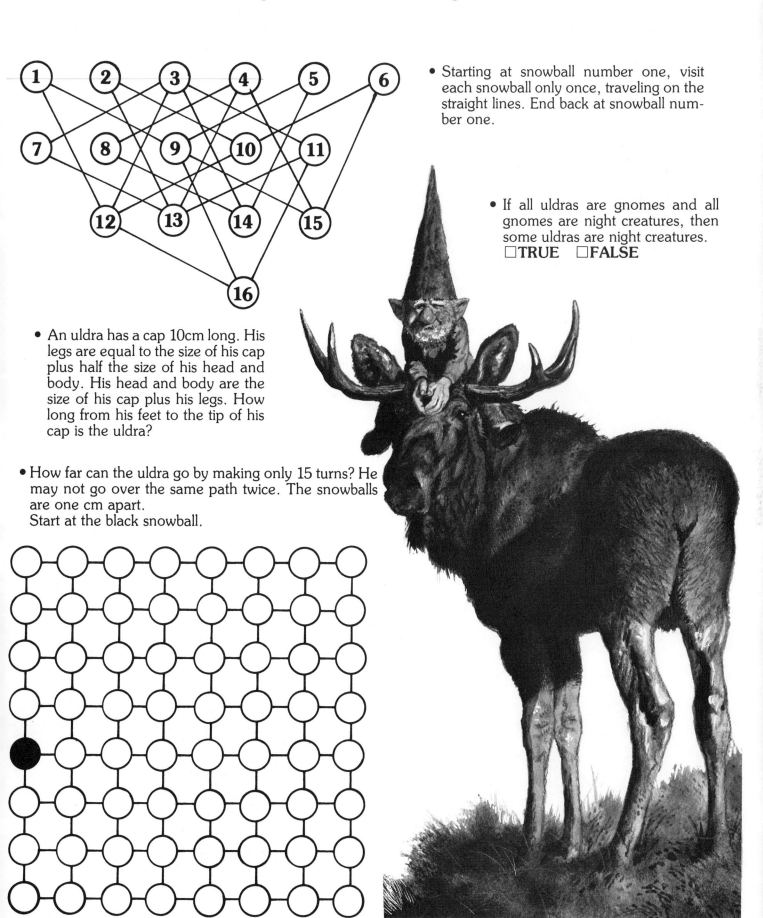

- Starting at snowball number one, visit each snowball only once, traveling on the straight lines. End back at snowball number one.

- If all uldras are gnomes and all gnomes are night creatures, then some uldras are night creatures.
☐TRUE ☐FALSE

- An uldra has a cap 10cm long. His legs are equal to the size of his cap plus half the size of his head and body. His head and body are the size of his cap plus his legs. How long from his feet to the tip of his cap is the uldra?

- How far can the uldra go by making only 15 turns? He may not go over the same path twice. The snowballs are one cm apart.
Start at the black snowball.

THE CARPENTRY LESSON

Each picture frame below has its component parts along side. Mark on the complete frame where the parts join.

GNOME PINBALL

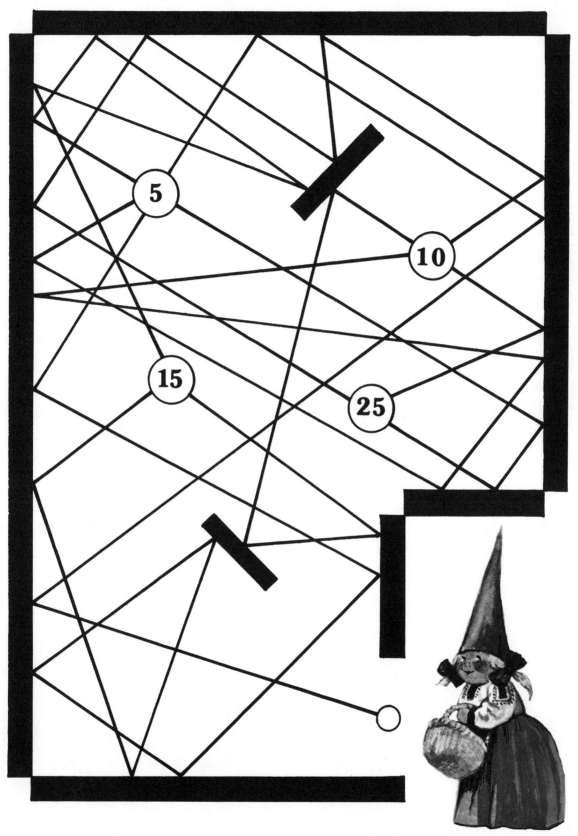

Starting at the gnome girl and following the lines as they bounce off the walls, can you reach an exact score of 100 points and then return to the girl without adding any points? When you hit a circled number you may take **any** path out of the circle except the one you came in on.

GNOME CROSSWORD PUZZLE

ACROSS

1. Pie_____ mode
4. _____ children live with their parents until they are 100 years old.
6. What *slitzweitz* means in the gnome language.
8. A gnome remedy for constipation.
10. Several trolls might have a confusing fight like this among themselves.
11. Result
13. Situated beneath the earth's surface, such as gnome dwellings.
14. After too much 107 Across, gnomes become _____: silly
16. Dissolute persons
17. Fabric
20. More recent
22. A flower possibly found in a garden gnome's garden.
23. French common soldier
25. What a gnome does when he awakens.
27. Tint
28. Hateful night creatures, admittedly malevolent, very often carry small shovels
30. Gnomes _____ cry wolf.
32. Gnomes have a close_____ with animlas: ties
33. Gnomes keep a _____ decoration on their table all year long.
35. Tea _____ drawn from white fiber of a walnut: medicine
37. Descriptive of a gnome tree house.
38. The shine of a gnome's silver bathroom mirror.
39. _____ Claus: gnome lookalike
41. Namesakes of a quilt maker on page 50.
43. Dune gnomes live under pine-tree _____ .
44. Gnome children are in their _____ before they stop wetting their beds.
45. Poor
47. Plants that reproduce by spores
49. Noun suffix describing gnomes: meaning small
50. A word that would apply to badgers and polecats
51. Pass along news
53. This is stiff and tough on gnomes.
54. Of, in Spanish
55. Thrushes and woodpeckers have these.
56. Poster of a beautiful girl
58. Gnomes _____ help injured animals.
59. This being likes to tease.
61. Times
62. A gnome's soccer _____ is a snowberry.
63. Snotgurgles love to _____ hold of a gnome.
64. Gnomes could smell one of these very easily: 2 words
66. British nobleman
68. After 63 Across, snotgurgles will torture a gnome to within an _____ of his life.
69. A gnome's _____ span is 400 years.
70. Man's nickname
72. The lyric poems that are the words to the music box tunes in every gnome dowry chest.
75. Oaf or dolt such as a troll
77. Extraordinary sense possessed by gnomes: abbr.
80. Gnomes never go where there might be a snotgurgle _____ a polecat.
81. Tomte and Thym
83. Boasts
84. Gnome twins call their father this.
85. Fill up
88. Plant of the lily family
90. Polecats could easily hypnotize these amphibians.
91. The gnome wife knits underwear, stockings, etc. from the hair of this animal.
93. Woman's name
95. Towns in Holland
97. Impudent
98. Most gnomes don't live near _____: cities
99. Eagle's nest
101. Directions on a printers proof meaning "let it stand."
103. Japanese Caucasians
104. Word to describe the fermented honey drink called mead dew.
105. Some gnome families reside in wind_____.
107. Gnome nightcap: beverage, 2 words
109. Asian rulers
110. _____beaver
112. *Heinzelmannchen* is the name given to gnomes by these people: Germans
113. Famous gamesman and author
114. Where trolls live and the only place they have power over gnomes.
116. These lead down to gnome homes: stairs
117. Indigo dyes used for gnome smocks
118. Respond
120. Supersonic transport: abbr.
121. This creature is stupid and unbelievably ugly.
122. _____ book
124. Gnome twins may be 2 boys or 2 _____ .
125. Hawaiian dances
127. Double curve moldings
128. This insect can smell the opposite sex up to 11 kilometers away.
130. These horses would never step on a gnome.
131. Prying, snooping
132. 10 Down is a gnome house

DOWN

1. Electrode
2. An abundant store such as the gnomes have for winter.
3. Stroll leisurely
4. A gnome captured by a snotgurgle is usually a_____.
5. Staring
6. Gnomes prefer being inside when these strong winds blow.
7. Dye the color of gnome caps
8. American Admiral George____
9. More naked
10. Gnomes keep a basket in their house for their pet field _____.
12. Man's name
13. Yearns
15. Affirmative replies
16. 100-year-old gnomes become _____: lustful and amorous
17. Gnomes love to sing with this bird.
18. When a gnome _____ he whistles a staccato tune taught to him by his father: falls ill
19. Gnomes make these openings in a cow's peritoneum when it gets "the sharps."
21. A good word to describe a party prior to gnomes' honeymoon trip.
22. Dune gnomes live under these trees.
23. Small openings
24. Emasculate
26. Finishing touch, pertaining to letters

60

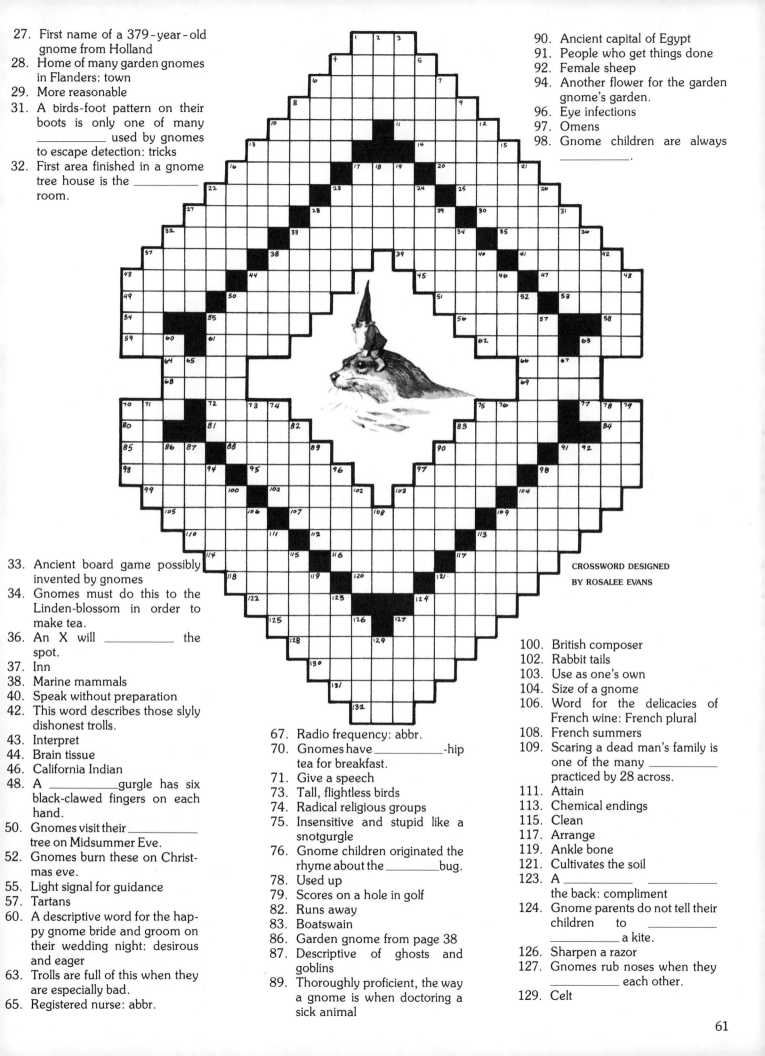

27. First name of a 379-year-old gnome from Holland
28. Home of many garden gnomes in Flanders: town
29. More reasonable
31. A birds-foot pattern on their boots is only one of many _____ used by gnomes to escape detection: tricks
32. First area finished in a gnome tree house is the _____ room.

33. Ancient board game possibly invented by gnomes
34. Gnomes must do this to the Linden-blossom in order to make tea.
36. An X will _____ the spot.
37. Inn
38. Marine mammals
40. Speak without preparation
42. This word describes those slyly dishonest trolls.
43. Interpret
44. Brain tissue
46. California Indian
48. A _____gurgle has six black-clawed fingers on each hand.
50. Gnomes visit their _____ tree on Midsummer Eve.
52. Gnomes burn these on Christmas eve.
55. Light signal for guidance
57. Tartans
60. A descriptive word for the happy gnome bride and groom on their wedding night: desirous and eager
63. Trolls are full of this when they are especially bad.
65. Registered nurse: abbr.

67. Radio frequency: abbr.
70. Gnomes have _____-hip tea for breakfast.
71. Give a speech
73. Tall, flightless birds
74. Radical religious groups
75. Insensitive and stupid like a snotgurgle
76. Gnome children originated the rhyme about the _____bug.
78. Used up
79. Scores on a hole in golf
82. Runs away
83. Boatswain
86. Garden gnome from page 38
87. Descriptive of ghosts and goblins
89. Thoroughly proficient, the way a gnome is when doctoring a sick animal

90. Ancient capital of Egypt
91. People who get things done
92. Female sheep
94. Another flower for the garden gnome's garden.
96. Eye infections
97. Omens
98. Gnome children are always _____.

CROSSWORD DESIGNED
BY ROSALEE EVANS

100. British composer
102. Rabbit tails
103. Use as one's own
104. Size of a gnome
106. Word for the delicacies of French wine: French plural
108. French summers
109. Scaring a dead man's family is one of the many _____ practiced by 28 across.
111. Attain
113. Chemical endings
115. Clean
117. Arrange
119. Ankle bone
121. Cultivates the soil
123. A _____ _____ the back: compliment
124. Gnome parents do not tell their children to _____ _____ a kite.
126. Sharpen a razor
127. Gnomes rub noses when they _____ each other.
129. Celt

SOLUTIONS

P. 1. (top) Let dwarf = X, gnome = Y, goblin = Z and the troll = A. X = Y + Z, Y = Z + A, and 2X = 3A. Let X = 12 then 24 = 3A, A = 8. X = 10 + 2, Y = 2 + 8 so X = 12, Y = 10, Z = 2 and A = 8. It would take five goblins to balance with a gnome.

(bottom) The gnome with the dirty face saw the gnome with a clean face and assumed that his face was the same. The gnome with the clean face saw the other gnome's dirty face and assumed that his face was also dirty. So he washed up before going home.

P. 5. The bottom picture differs from the top in these ways:
1. Girl missing from behind door
2. Pot missing from stove
3. Design on lady gnome's blouse is gone
4. Extra designs on base of oven
5. Logs stacked differently
6. Vase gone from shelf above door
7. Circle design missing from right-hand door

P. 6. (top) All of the tools will fit. The largest tool will fit the diagonal opening of the box even though it is slightly longer than the length of the opening.

(bottom) A seamstress mends the tears and a groom tends the mares.
The back of a clock.
The room for improvement.
They cell (sell) it.

P. 7. Third from the left, second row.

P. 8. (top) X = the number of years ago when the old gnome was as old as the nephew. Y = nephew's age now. 480 − X = Y, X − Y = 240, 2Y = 720 so Y = 360. The nephew is 360.

(bottom) Imp ate his share and left eight. His share was 1/3, so he must have eaten four and left eight. Tomte must have found 18 hazelnuts and Thym must have found 27, the original amount.

P. 9. 1.NO, 2.NO, 3.YES.

P. 10. (top) If it were his *widow* he wouldn't be alive.
They would be the same distance from the cave.
Just pluck the goose to get *down*.

Nobody said the rope was tied to anything else but his leg. Four minutes to fry both eggs (in the same pan, at the same time).

P. 11.

P. 12. (top) The gnome first takes an object from the basket labeled **"Hazelnuts and Blackberries."** As this basket is wrongly labeled, whatever is in that basket must indicate the actual contents. He puts the proper label on the first basket, then simply switches the other two labels to complete his task.

(bottom) The letters stand for: ten, twenty, thirty, forty, fifty, sixty, seventy—so the remaining two are (e)ighty and (n)inty.

P. 13. NOBODY CAN KEEP A SECRET FROM A GNOME.

P. 14. (top) 1.True 2.True 3.True 4.False 5.True 6.False 7.True 8.True
(bottom) **HAY**

P. 15 GNOMES NEVER HAVE HEART ATTACKS

P. 16. SIGHT
INNER
GNOME
HEMPS
TRESS

P. 18. (top) ACUPUNCTURE
(bottom) 1.Trolls 2.Dwarf 3.Goblin 4.Elf 5.Deer 6.Ant 7.Hornet 8.Otter

P. 19. Gnome Olie counted the second nut twice.

P. 20. (top) One longs to eat and the other eats too long.
(bottom) The traveler asked, "What directions would your brother give me?" The answer by *either* troll would give the correct answer. The liar would lie and the truthful one would say that his brother lied, so the traveler would take the opposite path given in the troll's response.

P. 21. A.7 B.4 C.11

P. 22. (top) The time is 4:10.
(bottom) **BRASS**: It is a mixture of elements.

P. 23.

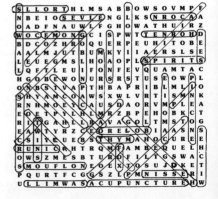

SOLUTIONS

P. 25.

P. 26. (top) **T E N**

(middle) Seven and five is *twelve*.

(bottom) He *juggled* them across with one always in the air.

P. 27. First one, top row.

P. 28. (top) 78 drink mead dew minus 48 = 30 who drink *only* mead dew. 71 drink fermented raspberries minus 48 = 23 who drink *only* fermented raspberries. Those who drink *only* mead dew (30) and those who drink *only* fermented raspberries (23) plus those who drink both (48) equal 101. *However,* only 100 were interviewed.

(bottom) There is the *same* amount of mead dew in the spiced gin as there is spiced gin in the mead dew. The first spoonful contains 100% spiced gin, the second 99% mead dew and 1% spiced gin (these proportions for example only).

P. 29.

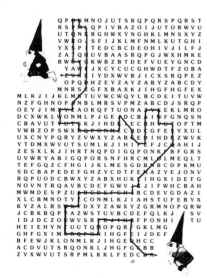

P. 30. (top) The time is 7:13, so Pimple appears to be innocent.

(bottom) **SWIMMING IS TOO RISKY FOR GNOMES.**

P. 31. (top) The gnome's relative was his *sister*.

(bottom)

P. 32. (top) **OAK SHOULD BE AVOIDED, DON'T STAND UNDER A WILLOW, THE PINE IS IN DANGER, BUT BEECH MAY BE SAFELY SOUGHT.**

(bottom)

P. 33

P. 34. (top) Second from the left, bottom row.

(bottom) Because he is titled.

P. 35. Middle picture, bottom row,

P. 36. (top) Tomte had 11 berries. Olie had 7 berries. Imp had 21, for a total of 39.

(bottom) **SNOW NAME OMEN WENT**

P. 37. PO (a river in Italy), POLE, POLECAT, OLE, OL, CAT, AT, ELF, ELFIN, FIN, IN, DWARF, WAR, FOR, OR, REST, TROLL, ROLL, LLAMA, LAM, AM, MA, MAGIC, CROW, ROW, OWL, ON, LONG, GNOME, NO, OMEN, MEN, ME, EN-DIVE, DIVE, MEND.

P. 38. (top) 1. Wartje, house gnome 2. Tomte, woodland gnome 3. Olie, dune gnome 4. Imp, farm gnome 5. Thym, garden gnome

(bottom) His grandson.

P. 39. BADGDEFIFCBEHKLIHGJK

P. 40. (top) HATCH
AURAE
TROLL
CALVE
HELEN

(bottom) **TROLLS
GOBLIN
BOLERO
RABBIT
SAWING
BUREAU
FLOWER
AIDING
FENNEL
CRADLE**

P. 41. (top) Go to rung 1 then back to the ground. Then proceed: 1,2,3,2,3,4,5,4,5,6,7,6,7, 8,9,8,9,—every rung has been used twice and the ground and top rung have been reached twice.

(bottom) The troll has the word *stop* lettered on the top rung.

P. 42. (top) **OLD PIMPLE IS A FEARSOME TROLL.**

(bottom) There is an equal amount of grey and black felt.

P. 43. 1.A3 2.B6 3.C9

P. 44. (top) E.

(bottom)

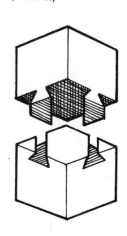

SOLUTIONS

P. 45. (top) Number 4, top row and number 2, bottom row.
(bottom) Number 2, top row and number 5, top row.

P. 46. (top) **1.OTTER, 2.FOX, 3.RABBIT, 4.DEER, 5.SPIDER, 6.FROG, 7.SQUIRREL, 8.POLECAT, 9.BADGER.**

(bottom) No. 2 does not matter because it is white. If No. 1 has a triangle, the answer is NO. If No. 3 is black, the answer is NO. If No. 1 is an oval and No. 3 is white, then no matter what No. 4 is, the answer is YES. The answer to question 1 is: Nos. 1 and 3.

P. 47.

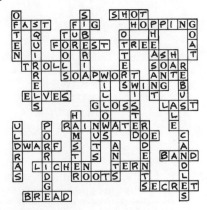

P. 48. (top) The gnome sets fire to the island downwind from him. As the fire burns, he follows it. The first fire burns out when it reaches the spot where the gnome's fire started, thus the gnome is saved.
(bottom) 36, 9 is ¾ of 12, 12 is ⅔ of 18, 18 is ½ of 36.

P. 49.

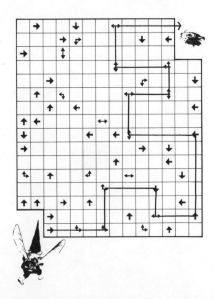

P. 50. It only takes four colors to color *any* map or chart using the method described.

P. 51. (top)

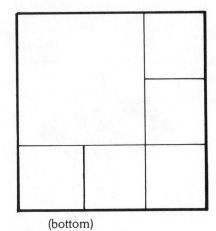

(bottom)

P. 52.

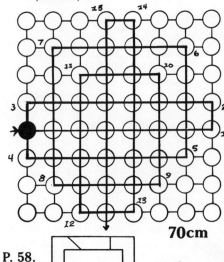

Divide this page with *three* straight lines so that each wooden bunny and each gnome twin occupies his own space. No line may enter this paragraph.

P. 53. (top) **G-O-A-W-A-Y-T-R-O-L-L**

(bottom) The gnome was born in 1680. Here are the dates associated with the questions: 1. 1513-1542 2. 1689-1725 3. 1588 4. 1666 5. 1661-1715 6. 1450 7. 1740-1780 8. 1630 9. 1682 10. 1603 11. 1649 12. 1215

P. 54. (top) **5**
(bottom) Picture one differs from the second picture in the following ways: 1. Cap is shorter. 2. Dot pattern on back of chair is missing. 3. Toilet paper roll is longer. 4. Lid knob is missing. 5. Handle is missing from gnome's hand. 6. Arm rest is missing. 7. Tool on floor is different.

P. 55. **23**

P. 56. (top) Lisa and Alice are sisters, Elsa is Lisa's sister-in-law.
(bottom) Make the pants and vest first.

P. 57. (top)
1-9-5-14-8-4-15-6-10-2-13-7-3-11-16-12-1
(top) TRUE
(middle) 80cm.

(bottom)

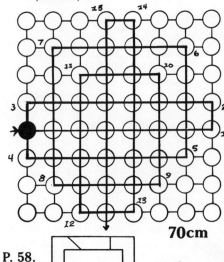

70cm

P. 58.

P. 59. 5-25-10-15-5-25-10-5-OUT

P. 61.